THE GREAT BOOK OF BANGTAN BOYS (BTS)

The Biography Of Each K-pop Idol. What You Need To Know As An Army.

SYLVIA SNOW

All rights reserved. No part of this publication may be reproduced, distributed, or transmitted in any form or by any means, including photocopying, recording, or other electronic or mechanical methods, without the prior written permission of the publisher, except in the case of brief quotations embodied in critical reviews and certain other noncommercial uses permitted by copyright law.

Copyright © SYLVIA SNOW, 2022.

Table Of Contents

CHAPTER ONE
- JIMIN

CHAPTER TWO
- RM

CHAPTER THREE
- V

CHAPTER FOUR
- JUNGKOOK

CHAPTER FIVE
- JIN

CHAPTER SIX
- J-HOPE

CHAPTER SEVEN
- SUGA

CONCLUSION
- MEMBERS RELATIONSHIP HISTORY

CHAPTER ONE

JIMIN

THE LIFE AND TIMES OF PARK JIMIN, KING OF KOREAN POP

Talent can be had for much less money than table salt. The difference between a talented person and a successful person is that the successful person puts in a lot of effort.

On the 13th of October, 1995 found Park Ji-min, also known as in Korean, was born in the Geumjeong District of Busan, South Korea. On June 13, 2013, he made his public debut as a member of Bangtan Sonyeondan, more commonly referred to as BTS. BTS is the most successful boy band to come out of South Korea.

Jimin had a happy childhood and is very close to his immediate family, which consists of his mother, father, and brother who is two years younger than he is. Jimin's childhood was spent playing video games and watching cartoons. When Jimin recalls his joyful experiences from his childhood, such as going to the park with his family, playing together, and eating their packed lunches, he can't help but feel a rush of happiness all over again.

Because of his generous nature, his family, neighbors, teachers, classmates, and friends all hold a very high opinion of him, and he was a very successful student when he was a child.

When he was younger, his childhood ambitions included a career in either singing or law enforcement. The man who raised him always had the notion that his son would go into the legal profession or work for the government at some point. Jimin, on the other hand, had the epiphany that he wanted to be a singer when he was still in middle school. He laid out his plans for the future and shared them with his parents.

When Jimin decided that he wanted to pursue his dream of becoming an idol, his parents supported him wholeheartedly and were very understanding of his decision.

Jimin had to start from a very low position. Jimin's character has been significantly influenced by the development of a strong feeling of self-reliance as well as responsibility as he has aged. It provided him with a lot of desire and the ability to push himself extremely hard to establish his future.

Jimin went to Haedong Elementary School and Yongsan Middle School in the city of Busan. Since then, Jimin has been putting in a lot of effort. He was a diligent and dedicated student.

From elementary school through high school, he was able to maintain a respectable GPA while still participating in extracurricular activities such as becoming a member of the student government. Math and Chemistry were two of his favorite courses, whereas he did poorly in History.

Jimin had eight years of training in popping and locking when he was in middle school. Rain, a Korean musician, has been a major influence on Jimin's hip-hop style. Just Dance Academy was his place of education. Jimin nearly gave up on his dancing training since his family is unable to pay the tuition for the classes. Despite this, his instructor agreed to let him continue without having him pay the remainder of the tuition.

In exchange, Jimin put up a lot of effort and kept going. In addition, Jimin enrolled at the Art Academy so that he could better prepare for the admission examinations for the Busan School of Arts.

Jimin was able to get into the Busan School of the Arts because of his talents and his dogged dedication. He received his undergraduate degree in modern and contemporary dance. He graduated at the top of his class and served as president for all nine years of his high school career.

Jimin was well-liked by his classmates. One of his teachers was instrumental in persuading him to try out for a role with a production company, which he ultimately did to maximize his potential and reach new heights.

As a direct consequence of this, BigHit Entertainment, a Korean entertainment firm, decided to accept Jimin as a trainee. Jimin made the journey to Seoul, Korea, in May 2012, and immediately enrolled in Korean Arts High School there. He finished his education at this institution with another notable student who is also a member of BTS, Kim Taehyung, also known as V. Jimin received his degree in 2014.

Jimin has added a Master of Business Administration in Advertising and Media degree from Hanyang Cyber University to his already excellent list of academic accomplishments.

A well-rounded Jimin is not defined just by their academic performance. In addition to that, Jimin is athletic. Jimin has shown that he is capable of running extremely quickly and jumping quite high at the Idol Star Athletics Championship.

At the 2014 ISAC, Jimin was a member of the pink squad that competed in football with Shinee's Minho, Infinite's Woohyun and Honya, EXO's Luhan and Xiumin, B2ST's Doojoon, Kikwang, and Yoseob, TEEN TOP's Ricky, 2 AM's Seulong, TASTY's Sorong, Surprise's Gongmyung,

Jimin used to be a member of the school's Billiards club, and he is highly skilled when it comes to playing billiards. In addition, Jimin was a dedicated member of the school's football club and played football for the school team.

Jimin has been training in martial arts for more than eight years now. He was trained in Kendo, a historic kind of Japanese martial art that is also known as Japanese fencing and derived from the art of swordsmanship. Jimin is a black belt in Taekwondo. His interest in karate was sparked by a single piece of equipment. In addition to that, he trained in the Korean martial art of Hapkido.

He was the only student in his year at Busan Arts School to get a scholarship to study martial arts in China, and he did so when he was a freshman there.

As Jimin prepared to make his debut as an official member of BTS, he encountered a great deal of competition. As Jimin, who has a background in modern contemporary dance, realized that the idol dance, which is mostly centered on hip hop style, presents a significant obstacle for him to overcome, he was put through a series of tests.

Jimin was the penultimate member of BTS to debut, although he had the least amount of training time because of his enthusiasm, hard work, and commitment.

Jimin puts in work at the gym whenever he has a moment to spare. Jimin had a tremendous amount of enthusiasm, and he yearned to dance all the time. To perfect his abilities, he limited his sleep to three hours a day and worked on his skills till one or two in the morning.

Jimin made his debut with BTS in the roles of primary dancer and lead singer. It was with the publication of their song "No More Dream" that he made his first appearance. Jimin has recorded four outstanding solo tracks, which have continued to get a wide variety of recognitions and set records across a variety of platforms. Songs such as "Lie," "Serendipity," "Promise," and "Filter" are all solo efforts by Jimin.

Jimin, along with the other members of his band BTS, has accomplished a great deal since the group's inception. Jimin has been singled out and honored for his contributions to music and performances on several occasions. Jimin was anointed as the next King of K-pop in August

2019. Along with the other members of the group, the President of South Korea bestowed upon him in 2018 the Hwagwan Order of Cultural Merit of the Fifth Class, which he shared with the other members of the group.

This genuine, kind spirit that Jimin never, ever forgets to give back, despite the many benefits that have been showered upon him. By making contributions on many occasions for the benefit of students who are struggling to make ends meet, he demonstrates the value that he places on education.

Between the years 2016 and 2018, Jimin donated a personal gift to the Hoedong Elementary School, which he attended. With this donation, he covered the price of school uniforms for every kid who graduated from the school before it was shut down.

In a similar vein, Jimin donated in April 2019 to the Busan Metropolitan City Office of Education 100 million won, which is equivalent to $88,000, for education improvement. 30 percent of which was donated to the university he attended in the past.

Jimin was responsible for the replacement of all 1200 desks and chairs at the Busan High School of the Arts on February 9, 2020. Because he made a contribution that was more significant outside of his location, his generosity is not restricted to his alma mater or the region in which he was born. Jimin was kind enough to give pupils in Jeolla Province a donation of one hundred million won.

CHAPTER TWO

RM

RM, ALSO KNOWN AS RAP MONSTER, IS THE LEADER OF THE BOY BAND BTS FROM SOUTH KOREA.

RM, previously known as Rap Monster, is a well-known rapper, composer, and producer from South Korea. He is most well-known for his membership in the hip-hop group known as "Bangtan Boys." His legions of devoted followers in South Korea also call him by the moniker "Rapmon." He was an exceptionally bright kid who performed very well in all of his classes.

However, he began rapping at an early age and eventually decided to pursue it as a profession. Before becoming a member of the 'Bangtan Boys,' he performed as a solo artist and sang with a few local bands in the area. After becoming a member of the 'Bangtan Boys,' he quickly rose through the ranks to become the group's primary rapper and lyricist, as well as its leader.

He has worked together with some of the most well-known rappers from both Korea and other countries to make music that has gained widespread attention on the internet. The coffee brand 'K'hawah' and a variety of other items from South Korea have both received his support.

Because of his talk program, 'Hot Brain: Problematic Men,' he is a well-known figure on South Korean television. In addition, he has been profiled in many South Korean publications as one of the country's most promising rappers. He is quite engaged on many social media platforms and has a significant following online.

RM (RAP MONSTER) Celebrates His Birthday on September 12th, 1994 (Virgo)

Yeoui-Dong, Seoul, South Korea is where he was born.

Quick Facts; He's Also Known As Kim Nam-Joon

- Age: 28, Males of the Age of 28 Years Old
- Family: Siblings: Kim Geong Min
- South Korea is the nation of birth.
- Height: 5 ft 11 inches (180 cm), 5 ft 11 inches Males
- Global Cyber University and Apgujeong High School have produced notable alumni.
- The ENFP personality type
- City: Seoul, in the South Korean Republic

CHILDHOOD & EARLY LIFE

Kim Nam-Joon, better known as Rap Monster, was born on September 12th, 1994 in the Ilsan-gu neighborhood of Goyang, South Korea. In Soul, he spent his childhood beside his younger sister, Kim Geong Min. When he was in elementary school, he was fascinated by those who wore uniforms and dreamed of working as a security guard for a housing organization.

He graduated with honors from Global Cyber University, where he studied broadcasting and performing art and received his degree. He achieved an impressive TOEIC score of over 900 and was among the top scorers on the national school test. Both of these accomplishments deserve praise. Additionally, he had a very high IQ.

In school, he was taught both his native tongue and Japanese. Outside of school, he picked up fluency in English by watching famous American comedies like "Friends." In addition, he spent some time as a student in New Zealand and learned English, which he thought to be a vital skill.

Because of the way he performed in school, his parents anticipated that he would soon start working a normal job. Despite this, he was able to persuade his parents to let him pursue rapping

17

as a full-time career because of his passion for the music he listened to and the friends he hung out with. While he was still in school, he was already penning songs that were highly successful and popular.

According to him, rapping helped him get over the stress of his academics, and the lyrics of his song "No More Dreams" were inspired by the days when he worked late into the night for his examinations. He said that rhyming helped him get over the stress of his studies.

CAREER

Kim Nam-Joon started as a solo artist under the stage name "Runch Randa" when he first began his career in the music industry. In 2008, he was a part of the South Korean hip-hop group Zico for a short period. At the time, Zico was one of the emerging stars in the South Korean hip-hop world. In addition to that, he was a member of the Korean hip-hop group known as "Daenamhyup" for some time.

Later on, in 2013, he became a member of the well-known K-pop group BTS, also called the Bangtan Boys, and after that, he became known as the "Rap Monster" among his devoted following. In June of 2013, he released his first single album with BTS under the title '2Cool 4 Skool,' which included the smash hit 'No More Dream.' After then, he became the leader of BTS and the primary rapper, in addition to writing the lyrics for a lot of singles that the group had released.

In addition to working with BTS, he has worked with several other Korean and international artists to create some of the most successful rap music tracks and videos that went viral between the years 2014 and 2016. These include "Please Don't Die" with Warren G, "Bucku Bucku " with the hip-hop group MFBTY's, and the soundtrack of "Fantastic Four" with Marvel. Other collaborations include "Bucku Bucku" with the hip-hop group MFBTY.

He has been on the talk program "Hot Brain: Problematic Men," in which he is one of five celebrities who debate contemporary social problems that are affecting today's young people. The show has been called "Hot Brain: Problematic Men."

Rap monster has been published in a lot of publications and is one of the featured artists in the Korean book named "HipHopHada," which is a collection of the most prominent Korean hip-hop artists. As one of South Korea's most promising rappers, he has also been featured in the American magazine XXL, which has written about him.

Kim Nam-Joon has been featured in a variety of advertisements and endorsements for Korean companies during his career. He now has the position of brand ambassador for the well-known 'K'hawah coffee brand, which is manufactured in South Korea.

He maintains an active presence across several social media platforms and has a sizable fan base both in South Korea and outside.

Both the song "Fantastic Feat" from the album "Fantastic Four" and the song "Reflection" from the album "Wings" have been recognized as successful singles in South Korean music charts.

His popular songs done in cooperation with other singers include "Perfect Christmas" with Jo Kwon, Lim Jeong-hee, Joohee, and Jungkook, as well as "Please Don't Die" with Warren G., which is a worldwide favorite.

In March 2015, he released a mixtape titled RM on the internet in the form of a digital download. The mixtape was published under the company Big Hit Entertainment.

A number of music videos, such as "School of Tears" (2012), "Adult Child" (2013), "Do You" (2014), and "Bucku Bucku" (2015), as well as his most recent music video, "Change," which was released in 2017, have been produced by him.

In addition to that, he has made guest appearances on the television series 4 Things Show – Rap Monster,' 'Hot Brain: Problematic Men,' 'Close-up Observation Diary on Idol: Find Me,' and 'Gura-Chacha: Time Slip – New Boy.'

AWARDS & ACHIEVEMENTS

At the Golden Disk Awards and the MelOn Music Awards in 2013, Rap Monster received recognition for their work. The following year, 2013, he was honored once again at both the Gaon Chart K-Pop Awards and the Seoul Music Awards.

PERSONAL LIFE

It is not known that Rap Monster is dating anyone in particular, and it is believed that he is single at present. In the past, he has been quoted as saying during an interview that if he ever had a girlfriend who was not involved in show business, he would have to apologize to her regularly due to his hectic schedule, which leaves him with no time for activities such as dating.

TRIVIA

Because he had such impressive dancing movements, the dance instructor at his school gave him the moniker "Dance Prodigy." Swinging his arms from side to side is one of his favorite moves to do while he's dancing.

Later on, his devoted followers began to refer to him as 'RapMon,' 'Leader Mon,' and even 'God of Destruction.' It was well known that he would always succeed in damaging items that his fellow rapper, "Suga," would then have to fix. In addition to this, he is prone to accidents and is often injured.

His bandmates in Bangtan Boys are known by the stage names Jin, Suga, J-Hope, Jimin, and V, respectively. Jungkook is also a member of the group.

Both Korean knife noodles and the video game Maple Story are among his top culinary and entertainment preferences, respectively.

He identifies as an agnostic and is a staunch advocate for the rights of LGBT people.

CHAPTER THREE

V

WHO IS SINGER V OF BTS? HIS EARLY LIFE, CAREER, AND PERSONAL LIFE, AS WELL AS HIS ACHIEVEMENTS

Kim Tae-Hyung, who was born on December 30, 1995, and is better known by his stage name V, is a performer from South Korea who is also a composer and actor. He is a member of the South Korean boy band BTS and sings in the group. Continue reading to get his whole life.

V is the stage name given to South Korean singer, composer, and dancer Kim Taehyung. He is sometimes known simply as V. Today, he is most well-known for his role as a prominent member of the well-known K-pop group Bangtan Boys (simply known as BTS).

V, or Tae as he is more often known, has a sizable fan following not just in South Korea but also in other countries across the world. This hip-hop singer is well-known for his strong voice as well as his youthful good looks. He conceived of and was instrumental in the production of the band's two most successful songs, "2 Cool 4 Skool" and "Boy in Luv."

His career began in the music business of South Korea, and within a short amount of time, he climbed to the top of the charts globally, marking yet another important achievement in K-pop for the country.

BTS has a large fan base, both online and offline, as shown by the fact that they have more than five million followers on their Twitter profile as of the year 2017. His devoted following is composed almost entirely of young women who find themselves unable to get enough of his endearing good looks and demeanor.

KIM TAEHYUNG: EARLY LIFE AND EDUCATION

Kim Tae-Hyung, better known as V, was born on December 30, 1995, in the Seo District of Daegu, South Korea. V spent most of his childhood in Geochang County. He has a younger brother and sister who are his younger siblings, making him the oldest of three children. When V was in primary school, her initial career goal was to become a professional singer.

To pursue a career as a saxophonist, he started taking lessons on the instrument while he was still in the early grades of middle school, with his father's encouragement. After doing well at an audition in Daegu, V was finally accepted into Big Hit Entertainment's training program.

V went on to get a degree in Broadcasting and Entertainment from Global Cyber University, which he attended immediately after he graduated from Korean Arts High School in 2014. He received his diploma in August 2020.

Since the year 2021, he has been a student at Hanyang Cyber University, where he is working toward obtaining a Master of Business Administration degree with a concentration in advertising and media.

Kim's adventure started when he and his current band member Jimin developed a remix of "Old School Love ft. Ed Sheeran" and released it on Soundcloud to celebrate their graduation. The song had Ed Sheeran as the featured artist.

After that, he became a member of Bangtan Boys in 2011, but it wasn't until 2013 that his membership was made publicly known by the band. He contributed to the writing, production, and composition of many songs, including "Hold Me Tight" and "Fun Boyz."

The combination of his melody and Jungkook's creative lyrics propelled the group's song "Stigma" to the tenth position on the Billboard World Digital Singles Chart, while it debuted at position number 26 on the Gaon Music Chart.

Kim is well-known for his rendition of Adele's song "Someone Like You," which helped him get a lot of attention and recognition. A number of accolades, including the Melon Music Awards, the Gaon Chart K-pop Awards, the Golden Disk Awards, and the Seoul Music Awards, have been bestowed to his band BTS.

In 2016, V made his debut in the acting world, marking his expansion into yet another subgenre of the entertainment business. It was in the historical drama 'Hwarang: The Poet Warrior Youth' that he made his acting debut on KBS2. In addition to that, he was the one who composed and arranged the film's catchy music.

Kim Taehyung is one of those persons who appear from nowhere and very immediately take over the internet by storm with their popularity. In addition to being a phenomenal singer, composer, and keyboardist, he is also just beginning his career as an actor.

Because he has a wide range of skills, the future seems promising for him. Not only is he very talented, but he also serves as the public face of his band and is without a doubt one of the most well-known and successful K-pop performers of all time.

KIM TAEHYUNG: NET WORTH

V is a singer, composer, and actor from South Korea who has accumulated a net worth of $20 million. His role as a vocalist with the South Korean boy band BTS, commonly known as the Bangtan Boys, is mostly responsible for his notoriety.

Touring brought in a total of $170 million for the band in 2019. Metallica was the only band to earn more than the others combined. Between June 2019 and June 2020, the members of BTS earned a collective $50 million, or around $7 million for each member, thanks primarily to the profits generated from their touring activities.

The management business of South Korean boy band BTS, Big Hit Entertainment, made its debut on the South Korean stock market on September 28, 2020. The market capitalization of the firm was $4.1 billion while trading for the first time today. It was the third biggest stock market debut in South Korea during the last three years.

Big Hit founder Bang Si-Hyuk completed the day of the business's initial public offering (IPO) with a net worth of $1.4 million. Bang Si-Hyuk owns 43% of the company. One month before the first public offering, Bang distributed 68,385 shares of the firm to each member of the group. This was in preparation for the IPO.

When the first day of trading for the firm was over, each of the seven members realized that they had holdings that were worth $7.9 million.

KIM TAEHYUNG: PERSONAL LIFE

Kim Taehyung, also known as V, was born on December 30th, 1995 in the city of Daegu, which is located in South Korea. There, he spent his childhood with his two younger siblings, Kim Eon Jin and Kim Jeong Gyu, both of whom are his sister and brother, respectively.

He is highly devoted to his family, and he emphasizes over and again that his father is the one who most inspires him. His family has been in agriculture for generations, and he comes from a background that is not very affluent. His family has always been there to provide him with the encouragement and support he needs to pursue a career in the entertainment industry.

He claims that he is a highly romantic guy, despite the fact that he does not have a significant other at the moment. It is reported that he is obsessed with fragrances and that his interest in music goes back to when he was still in school. His profession is now his primary priority, and as a result, it is where the majority of his attention is being directed right now.

V boasts a baritone singing voice that has had a generally favorable critical reaction, with particular acclaim for his vocal range and "husky" tone. V also owns a singing voice that has been described as having an operatic quality. It was his performance of his solo song "Stigma" that brought him greater vocal fame.

During this performance, he was lauded for his falsettos, which displayed his vocal range and his distinctive musicality. Blanca Méndez, a music reviewer, called V's tonality on "Singularity," the first track of BTS' Love Yourself: Tear (2018) album, a key "tone setter" on the album.

Along the same lines, Katie Goh of Vice referred to it as "one of V's greatest vocal performances." It was noted that V has no issue delivering incredibly calming, deep tones that are a significant aspect in the overall sound for BTS. It was also mentioned that V's lower range is an important component of BTS' music.

His passion for jazz as well as classical music has had a significant impact on V's ability to create music. His influences include people like Eric Benet and Ruben Studdard, among others.

As a performer, V is noted for having a style that is characterized by its "duality," which refers to his ability to inspire a variety of emotions while on stage. When analyzing V's performance of "Singularity" during the Love Yourself: Speak Yourself World Tour, the British writer Rhian Daly wrote for NME that V's motions were "precise and intentional."

Daly made this observation, especially when examining V's rendition of the song. Crystal Bell, a contributor for MTV, said how V's performances often interact with live cameras in concert settings and how he employs them to produce subtle reactions while he is performing.

Following in the footsteps of Brad Pitt, Hrithik Roshan, and Robert Pattinson, BTS

V IS CROWNED THE MOST HANDSOME MAN OF 2021.

Kim Tae-Hyung, better known around the globe by his stage name V, is a member of "BTS," which is widely considered to be the most successful band in the world. In addition to being a composer and actor, he also performs vocals for the band. He is also a multi-instrumentalist. Because of his good looks and impeccable sense of style, he is very well-known all over the globe.

At the age of 18, he made his professional debut with BTS in June 2013. Since that time, his singing and voice have received less attention than his looks and charisma in the media. He is exceptionally attractive and does not attempt to hide the fact that he is. Even in more trendy attire, he flaunts his attractiveness.

The results of the poll that was carried out by Besttopper.com have determined that V is the Most Handsome Man of 2021. When it comes to handsomeness, he has topped the list despite the presence of some big names from around the world, and when it comes to achievements up to this point, he has topped the list even more.

The names Brad Pitt, Hrithik Roshan, Henry Cavill, Tom Cruise, and Robert Pattinson are among those that appear on the list, along with many more.

It has no novel ideas or concepts. This recognition came from the YouTube channel "Top 10 World," which ranked V number one on their list of the Most Handsome Men of 2020. Additionally, he was victorious against some of the most well-known actors and musicians in the Bollywood and Hollywood entertainment industries.

Therefore, being complimented on his good looks is nothing new for V. to experience. It is quite an accomplishment in and of itself that he has been chosen as the World's Most Handsome

Man for the second year running in a row now since this is the case every year.

DO YOU WANT TO KNOW MORE ABOUT THE GREAT KPOP IDOLS OF OUR TIME? ARE YOU AN ARMY AND YOU WANT TO KNOW MORE ABOUT BTS?

I have an incredible book that will educate you on more than three hundred facts about BTS that you were previously unaware of.

CLICK HERE TO GET BTS FACTS

CHAPTER FOUR

JUNGKOOK

(SINGER, SONGWRITER, AND VOCALIST FOR THE SOUTH KOREAN BOY BAND 'BTS'; ALSO THE YOUNGEST MEMBER OF THE GROUP)

Jungkook, whose birth name is Jeon Jeong-guk, is a member of the musical band known as Bangtan Boys or BTS. He is the main singer, as well as a dancer and a rapper. This hip-hop group also includes Kim Taehyung, Rap Monster, Jimin, Jin, Suga, and J-Hope.

He is the newest addition to the group and the youngest member overall. The young guy has been a member of BTS since 2013, and he is well-known for his ability to inspire and motivate audiences at concerts with his energetic rapping and dancing performances.

Because Jungkook has a great deal of skill, although he is still relatively young, he has amassed an enormous fan base and is famous in many Asian nations in addition to South Korea. This popularity is not limited to South Korea. And it's important to point out that the majority of his songs and videos have become massive successes in their own right.

In addition to his skills as a singer, rapper, and dancer, Jungkook has an endearing and magnetic personality. His charming appearance is another factor that has contributed to his success. It comes as a surprise that the media is unable to provide any information on his romantic relationships.

Jungkook's Birthday: September 1, 1997 (Virgo)
Born in: Busan, which is located in South Korea

QUICK FACTS
- Age: 25 Years Old
- Family: Siblings: Jeon Jung Hyun (Older Brother)

- South Korea is his nation of birth.
- Height: 5 feet 10 inches (178 cm), 5 feet 10 inches males
- Global Cyber University and the School of Performing Arts in Seoul have produced notable alumni.
- ISFP is the personality type.
- Busan is located in South Korea.

CAREER

At the age of 13, Jungkook tried out for the television talent show known as "Superstar K," but he was ultimately not selected. He was fortunate enough to get offers from eight different talent agencies as he was driving home. Soon after, he was given a contract by Big Hit Entertainment.

At the age of 14, Jungkook began his training in dancing at Movement Lifestyle. In the year 2013, he joined the boy band BTS and released his first single, titled "No More Dream," which was included in the album titled "2 Cool 4 Skool."

After this, Jungkook, along with the other members of his band, created a string of critically acclaimed albums and singles. In addition, the band has performed many stage concerts and has even been to many other countries on tour.

It is possible to gauge the band's level of success by looking at the size of its fan base as well as the band's popularity on a global scale. It should also be noted that the boy band has won several honors up to this point in time. To name just a few of the accolades it has received, we may mention the Melon Music Award, the Golden Disk Award, the Seoul Music Award, and the Bonsang Award.

When it comes to Jungkook's solo ventures, he has worked along with several prominent Korean singers and political figures to create the song "One Dream One Korea." This song portrays the bond between South Korea and North Korea as well as the desire for the two countries to become one. In addition, Jungkook appeared in the music video for "I'm Da One" by Jo Kwon in the year 2012.

Jungkook has also made guest appearances on many different television series. In 2014, he was a guest on three different episodes of the show 'BTS China Job.' Two years later, he participated in many television productions, such as "Flower Boy Bromance," "Special MC in Music Core," and "National Idol Singing Contest." In addition, the singer and dancer participated in the reality show 'Flower Crew' in the same year, with other notable celebrities such as Jo Se-ho, Yoo Byung-Jae, and Ki Min-Seok.

PERSONAL LIFE

On September 1st, 1997 in Busan, South Korea, Jungkook was given the name Jeon Jeong-guk at the time of his birth. In addition to attending the

Seoul School of Performing Arts, he received his education at Baek Yang Middle School.

In February 2017, the ambitious musician received their diploma. It is also stated that Jungkook is an accomplished chef. In addition to his many other interests, he enjoys painting and playing games, particularly soccer.

At the moment, Jungkook lives in the same house as his parents and his elder brother, Jung Hyun. Aside from this one fact, there is not a great deal of information available about the singer's family.

CHAPTER FIVE

JIN

KIM SEOK-JIN
(A MEMBER OF THE BOY BAND "BTS" ALSO REPRESENTING SOUTH KOREA)

Kim Seok-jin, better known by his stage name "Jin," is a singer-songwriter hailing from South Korea. He is also a member of the well-known seven-member K-pop boy band "BTS" from South Korea. After being discovered by "Big Hit Entertainment," Jin made his way into the music business and finally made his debut with "BTS" on the band's first studio album, which was titled "2 Cool 4 Skool."

His first co-produced tune, titled "Awake," was a solo single that was included on "BTS's" second album, titled "Wings." Jin's second solo effort was the song 'Epiphany,' which later became a part of the compilation album 'Love Yourself:

Answer' by 'BTS' and climbed to the top of various foreign charts, including the number four slot on the 'Billboard World Digital Singles Chart.' As a member of the band 'BTS,' he has gained notoriety all around the globe.

The band is well-known for its worldwide impact and has achieved new levels of success throughout its career. As a member of 'BTS,' Jin, along with the other band members, has been presented with several accolades and awards.

One of them is the fifth-class 'Hwagwan Order of Cultural Merit,' which was presented to the band by President Moon Jae-in of South Korea. In addition to hosting programs including "KBS Song Festival" and "Music Bank," Jin is a member of the boy band BTS and has worked with V, another member of the group, on the song "It's Definitely You."

Kim Seok-jin
The 4th of December, 1992 is his birthday (Sagittarius)

Gwacheon-Si, South Korea, Is Where I Was Born.

A Few Quick Facts
- Age: 29, Males of the Age Group 29 Years Old
- Siblings: Kim Seok Jung
- South Korea is his nation of birth.
- Height: 5 feet 10 inches (178 cm), 5 feet 10 inches males
- Notable Alumni: Hanyang Cyber University, Konkuk University

CHILDHOOD AND EARLY LIFE

Kim Seok-jin was born on December 4th, 1992 in the city of Gwacheon, which is located in the province of Gyeonggi-do in South Korea. His family consists of his mother, his father, who is the CEO of a firm, and his older brother, Kim Seok Jung. His father is the patriarch of the family. His older brother is said to have been the one who initiated him into the world of hip-hop, according to the reports.

The name of Jin's high school was "Bosung High School." On February 22, 2017, he received his degree in art and performance from "Konkuk University," where he fulfilled his graduation requirements. At first, Jin was interested in working for his father's business.

On the other hand, he entered the entertainment business after being scouted for his attractiveness by the South Korean entertainment firm known as "Big Hit Entertainment" when he was out on the street. This led to his entry into the industry. During that time, Jin was pursuing his education in the performing arts.

CAREER

On June 13, 2013, Jin made his debut with the boy band BTS as one of the group's four singers. "2 Cool 4 Skool" was the name of their first single album.

Jin is responsible for singing on the solo track "Awake," which was included on the album "Wings," which was published in 2016 by "BTS." It was the first single that he released that he had co-produced. Along with Slow Rabbit, "Hitman" Bang, RM, J-Hope, and June, he contributed to the song's writing as a co-writer.

The song peaked at number 31 on the Gaon Music Chart and number 6 on the Billboard World Digital Singles Chart respectively. After that, in December of the same year, Jin published a Christmas version of the song on the platform known as "SoundCloud."

"It's Definitely You" was sung by Jin and V, both of whom are members of the boy band BTS. It was published as a part of the original soundtrack of the South Korean television series 'Hwarang: The Poet Warrior Youth,' which was also the source of its inspiration. Jin was given a nomination for the "Best OST Award" at the

"Melon Music Awards" in 2017 as a result of the song.

"Epiphany" was the name of the singer's second solo performance. On August 9, 2018, it was made available online for the very first time as a teaser for the then-upcoming compilation album of 'BTS' named 'Love Yourself: Answer.' On August 24 of that year, a complete version of the song was eventually made available as part of a compilation CD and was published.

The song, which "Billboard" referred to as having a "building pop-rock melody," climbed all the way up to number 4 on the "Billboard World Digital Singles Chart" after reaching number 30 on the "Gaon Music Chart," number 5 on the "K-pop Hot 100" chart in South Korea, and number 30 on the "Gaon Music Chart."

Additionally, he worked along with Jungkook, who is also a part of "BTS." They came out with a new rendition of the song "So Far Away," which was first presented to the public by "BTS" member Suga (Agust D) on the self-titled mixtape that August D published under his name.

In addition, Jin has sung cover versions of songs originally performed by other singers. These renditions of the songs may be found on Jin's "SoundCloud" page.

These include 'In Front of the Post Office in Autumn by Yoon Do-Hyun, which was released on June 7, 2018, as well as a solo cover of 'Mom' by Ra.D, which was released on May 7, 2015; 'I Love You' by Mate, which was released on December 3, 2015; and 'Mom' by Ra.D, which was released as a solo cover on May 7, 2015.

Jin has contributed to the writing of a number of songs that have been included in a variety of albums released by BTS throughout the years. These include the track titled "Outro: Circle Room Cypher" from the album "2 Cool 4 Skool" (2013), "Outro: Love Is Not Over" and "Boyz with Fun" from the album "The Most Beautiful

Moment in Life, Part 1" (2015), "Love Is Not Over" from the album "The Most Beautiful Moment in Life: Young Forever" (2016), and "Awake" from the album "Wings" (2016).

Jin has served as a co-host on several different television music shows. These include 'Inkigayo,' which was shown on 'SBS' in 2016, 'M Countdown,' which was broadcast on both 'Mnet' and 'KBS2' in 2016 and 2017, and 'Music Bank,' which was broadcast on 'KBS2' in 2018.

Jin also had an appearance on the South Korean reality-documentary program 'Law of the Jungle,' which is broadcast on 'SBS,' in 2017. Additionally, Jin co-hosted the annual South Korean music show 'KBS Song Festival,' both in 2017 and 2018.

Based on the results of a survey conducted by 'Gallup Korea' in 2018, Jin was ranked as the tenth most well-known idol in the South Korean market. In the same year, Jin and his older brother opened a restaurant in Seoul known as

"Ossu Seiromushi," which was inspired by Japanese cuisine.

In the same year, in October, Jin and the other members of the band 'BTS' were awarded the fifth-class 'Hwagwan Order of Cultural Merit' by South Korean president Moon Jae-in. Over the years, the band has received many awards and honors, and as of 2019, the band also holds seven 'Guinness World Records.'

FAMILY & PERSONAL LIFE

In 2018, Jin purchased a luxurious property in South Korea that was estimated to be worth $1.7 million US dollars. Despite this, he continues to share a home in Hannam-dong, Seoul, with the other members of his band. In December 2018, he celebrated his birthday by donating supplies to the "Korean Animal Welfare Association." These supplies included food, blankets, and dishes.

Additionally, he donated 321 kilograms of food to the non-profit organization "Korea Animal Rights Advocates" (KARA), which also supports animal welfare in Korea. Both of these organizations are dedicated to improving the conditions of animals in Korea.

Cooking, eating, taking care of dogs, snowboarding, and playing video games are some of Jin's favorite things to do in his spare time. In addition to that, he is the host of his very own "mukbang" program called "Eat Jin," on which he is sometimes accompanied by other members of "BTS," including Suga, Jimin, and Jungkook.

At the moment, Jin is a postgraduate student at the 'Hanyang Cyber University,' which is located in China. There, he studies topics other than music.

CHAPTER SIX

J-HOPE

J-HOPE (RAPPER)

J-Hope is a South Korean singer-songwriter, rapper, and dancer. He was born under the stage name Jung Ho-Seok.

The fact that he was in the boy band Bangtan Boys brought him most of his fame. He has released the studio albums "Dark & Wild," "Wings," "Wake Up," and "Youth" with the band, in addition to the mini-albums "Skool Luv Affair," "The Most Beautiful Moment in Life," and "Love Yourself: Her."

J-Hope, in collaboration with Bangtan Boys, has been a contributing member to many successful tunes, including "Miss Right," "Danger," "I Need U," "Run," "Epilogue: Young Forever," "Save me," and "Not Today," to mention a few.

As a solo artist, the South Korean vocalist is also responsible for the publication of the song "1 VERSE."

J-Hope has been on several different variety programs, some of which include 'After School Club,' 'American Hustle Life,' 'Weekly Idol,' 'Idol Star Athletics Championships,' 'The Boss is Watching,' 'National Idol Singing Contest,' and 'God's Workplace.'

When it comes to his honors and awards, the South Korean artist and his band were given the title of "New Artist of the Year" at the 2013 Golden Disk Awards, the 2013 MelOn Music Awards, the 2014 Gaon Chart K-Pop Awards, and the 2014 Seoul Music Awards. All of these accolades and awards took place in 2013.

J-HOPE
The 18th of February, 1994 is my birthday (Aquarius)
Ilgok-Dong, Gwangju, and South Korea are the places where he was born.

A Few Quick Facts
- Nick Name: Hobi
- In addition to these names: Jung Ho-Seok
- Age: 28, Males of the Age of 28 Years Old
- Mejiwoo is one of the family's siblings (Sister)
- Rappers K-Pop Singers
- Height: 5 feet 10 inches (178 cm), 5 feet 10 inches males
- Global Cyber University Has Produced Some Notable Alumni
- Gwangju is located in South Korea.

CAREER

In 2010, representatives from Big Hit Entertainment were present at big national castings when they made their first discovery of J-Hope.

After some time had passed, he finally signed his first contract for pre-debuts with the other members who had been chosen.

After that, he became the first trainee for Bangtan Boys, and in June 2013, he was finally accepted into the band as a full-fledged member. The band is completed by Jin, Suga, RM, Jimin, V, and Jungkook as the remaining members.

J-hope made his first appearance in the music industry in 2013 with the release of the track "No More Dream," which was included on the Bangtan Boys' first studio album, titled "2 Cool 4 Skool."

Since that time, the South Korean singer and the other members of his band have released a great number of studio albums, such as "Youth," "Wake Up," "Wings," and "Dark & Wild," as well as a great number of mini-albums, such as "Love Yourself: Her," "The Most Beautiful Moment in Life" (Part 1 & 2), and "O! RUL8,2?"

These albums and mini-albums each have a number of successful songs, including "Hold Me Tight," "Butterfly," "House of Cards," "My

City," "Love Is Not Over," "Am I Wrong," and "Whalien 52," to mention just a few examples.
The South Korean singer launched his solo career with the release of his first song, which was named "1 VERSE" and was released on December 21, 2015.

At the moment, J-Hope is participating in the production of songs for BTS with his other band members. Now, he is making preparations to release his debut mixtape under his name in 2018.

PERSONAL LIFE

J-Hope was originally given the name Jung Ho-Seok when he was born on February 18, 1994, in the city of Gwangju in South Korea.
Mejiwoo, his elder sister, is a popular figure on Instagram and a well-known Instagram personality.

Regarding the love life of the South Korean artist, the media has no information to provide about her relationships with other people.

In a similar vein, information on his school history, family history, and the identities of his parents cannot be found on the internet.

BTS has become more than just a band; they are a phenomenon that has enthralled the world with their contagious music and motivational message of self-acceptance and love. I take you on a tour through their early years in South Korea and their quick ascent to international prominence in this book.

Don't pass up the chance to discover more about one of the most well-known and influential bands in history.

CLICK HERE TO GET "THE WORLD OF BTS" BOOK

CHAPTER SEVEN

SUGA

SUGA IS A MEMBER OF THE RAP GROUP BOY BAND BTS FROM SOUTH KOREA. SUGA IS ALSO A RAPPER.

Aside from rapping and writing songs, Min Yoon-gi is also a record producer and composer. BTS, a popular South Korean pop group, counts him as one of its most renowned members.
Additionally, he has released many tracks under his name.

Before becoming a member of the K-pop group BTS, Yoon-gi was active in the underground rap scene. When he first began writing music, he was still a very small child.
More than 60 of his tracks have been released to the public.

Yoon-gi has been an indispensable member of 'BTS' ever since the band first introduced him to the public.

He is a multi talented individual who is capable of writing music, composing music, and mixing music.

Fans often refer to him by the nickname "Suga." Yoon-gi rose to prominence as a result of the phenomenal success of the band BTS. He is the one who millions of music fans all around the globe have their eyes on and their hearts beat faster for. He has a significant following among adolescents.

Suga's Birthday: March 9, 1993 (Pisces)
Buk District, Daegu, South Korea is where he was born.
A Few Quick Facts
- Other Names for This Person: Min Yoon-Gi
- He's 29 years,

- Height: 5 feet 9 inches (175 centimeters), 5'9" males
- Schools like Apgujeong High School and Global Cyber University have produced notable alumni.
- Daegu is located in South Korea.

CHILDHOOD & EARLY LIFE

Min Yoon-gi was born into a household of limited means on March 9, 1993, in the city of Daegu in South Korea. There is a sibling that is older than he is.

In the beginning, Yoon-gi went to a school called 'Taejeon Elementary School.' After that, he enrolled in "Gwaneum Middle School" and "Apgujeong High School." He attended the so-called "Global Cyber University" and graduated with a degree in Broadcasting Performing Art.

At the age of twelve, Yoon-gi was a fan of hip-hop music and would listen to songs like

"Ragga Muffin" by Stony Skunk and "Fly" by Epik High.

The fact that he saw hip-hop to be distinct from mainstream music served as a major motivation for him to explore the hip-hop musical genre.
At the juvenile age of 13, he began writing music for various ensembles.

Yoon-gi got his first job in the music industry when he was 17 years old and began working at a recording studio. During his time there, he expanded his knowledge in music composition and arrangement, and he also began his career as a rap musician.

At first, his parents did not provide a lot of support for the job path he decided to pursue. However, as time went on, they came to embrace his decision and were proud of him for it.

CAREER

When Min Yoon-gi first began his music career, he was a member of the underground hip-hop group known as "D-Town."

During his appearances, he was known by the stage moniker "Gloss." This was the exact way his name was rendered when translated into English. In 2010, he released the song "518-062," which was a commemorative song for the "Gwangju Uprising." This song was published when he was working with "D-Town." Additionally, he can be seen performing as a dancer in the music video for "I'm The One" by Jo Kwon.

Min Yoon-gi made his public debut in 2013 as a member of the South Korean boy band 'Bangtan Boys,' also known simply as 'BTS.' Big Hit Entertainment, which is also an entertainment firm, was responsible for the formation of the band.

When Yoon-gi joined 'BTS,' he began performing under the stage name "Suga."

The first two syllables of the word "shooting guard" were used to create the moniker for this position.

Yoon-gi has a deep appreciation for the game of basketball, which he played at the collegiate level as a shooting guard.

The band made their debut in June 2013, with the song "No More Dream," which was included on their first studio album, titled "2 Cool 4 Skool."

Yoon-gi is responsible for the composition of a lot of 'BTS' tunes.

"BTS" released two albums in 2014: "Wake Up" in Japan and "Dark & Wild" in South Korea. Both albums were released in 2014. Yoon-gi is the songwriter behind a lot of BTS's most popular songs, including "Jump," "Tomorrow," and "Like."

He wrote songs that were included on the band's critically acclaimed albums "Wings" and "The Most Beautiful Moment in Life, Part 1." His songwriting received a lot of praise, and it was a big reason why 'BTS' was able to achieve so much success.

The band has given performances on prestigious occasions including the "Billboard Music Awards" and the "Mnet Asian Music Awards."

At the 2017 "Billboard Music Awards," the K-pop group "Bangtan Boys" was recognized as the "Top Social Artist," making them the first K-pop group ever to get this honor.

In the year 2016, Min Yoon-gi launched his solo career and published his first mixtape on "SoundCloud" with the pseudonym "Agust D."

He arrived at the pseudonym by transposing the letters in the words "DT" and "Suga." His hometown, Daegu Town, is often referred to by its shortened version, 'DT.'

Yoon-gi spoke up about his struggles with anxiety and depression in this album. He also discussed his fear of social situations.

According to 'Fuse TV,' it was ranked as one of the best 20 mixtapes of the year 2016.

In 2017, Yoon-gi was the one who came up with the music for the artist Suran's song "Wine."

This song was quite popular among the younger generation in Korea. In December 2017, it was recognized as the finest "Soul/R&B" single at the "Melon Music Awards," where it also achieved the position of reaching second place on the "Gaon Digital Chart."

Because of his contributions to this song, Yoon-gi was given the "Hot Trend Award."

Yoon-gi relaunched his mixtape in February 2018, making it available for both purchase and streaming.

Following the album's reissue, it achieved a level of popularity that was previously unheard of.

It peaked at number three on the ``Billboard World Albums Chart" and number five on the 'Heatseekers Albums Chart' respectively.

In addition to this, it moved up the "Top Album Sales Chart" to position number 74.

Yoon-gi's first album as a solo artist, which was released under the alias "Agust D," debuted at position number 46 on the "Emerging Artists" list. There are now more than 60 songs that have been registered under Min Yoon-gi's name.

PERSONAL LIFE

Min Yoon-gi is single.
He has a long history of being an outspoken advocate for the LGBTQ+ community.
He has been open and honest about his struggles with depression.

There is a charitable side to Yoon-gi that comes out sometimes. He had pledged that if he ever got famous as a musician, he would provide his supporters with free pork. Yoon-gi, a member of the boy band BTS, celebrated his 25th birthday by donating beef to 39 different orphanages as part of the "Army" fans.

TRIVIA

Writing lyrics is an effective treatment for depression and stress.

Within an hour and a half, he had written the song "Like It." In spite of the fact that he has a laid-back personality, he works quite hard while writing music. He writes music every day, regardless of where he is or what he is doing, whether it be in a restroom or a waiting area. He enjoys writing poems about things that happen in everyday life.

He enjoys sleeping, being in areas with less noise, and being in locations with fewer people.

The other members of his band call him "Grandpa" rather often.

Min Yoon-gi hates dancing.
His interests outside of work include snapping pictures, reading comic books, and playing video games. He is enthusiastic about basketball.
He is well-versed in many Korean varieties, but his Japanese and English aren't quite as strong as their counterparts.

The character trait of Yoon-gi is of being truthful and forthright.
When younger members of his team make errors, he is direct with their words and reprimands them for their actions.

His song lyrics revolve around topics that are brimming with vitality and optimism.
His philosophy on life is summed up in the phrase "Let's live while having pleasure.

There is a big difference between playing music as a pastime and doing it professionally.

CONCLUSION

MEMBERS RELATIONSHIP HISTORY

Who exactly are the members of BTS dating? Learn all there is to know about the girlfriends of BTS members Jungkook, Jin, RM, Suga, Jimin, V, and J-Hope. The members of BTS have kept their dating life a well-guarded secret.

However, since photographs of BTS' V and BLACKPINK's Jennie are going viral on social media, here is a look at the reported list of girlfriends for Jungkook, Jin, RM, Suga, Jimin, V, and J-Hope.

BTS MEMBERS V, JUNGKOOK, JIN, RM, SUGA, JIMIN & J-HOPE'

Members of the K-pop group BTS and their girlfriends: Jungkook, Jin, RM, Suga, Jimin, V, and J-Hope keep their personal lives, including their romantic relationships, secret. BTS ARMY is very interested in learning more about Korean stars' personal life, especially the women in their lives, as Korean stars continue to gain followers all over the globe.

Recently, relationship speculations between V and BLACKPINK's Jennie surfaced when images of the two women together on Jeju Island were published online. V is a member of BLACKPINK. The two celebrities have not yet commented on the reports by denying or confirming them.

While we wait to hear from V and Jennie about their relationship, this is what we know about the dating lives of members of BTS:

WHO IS V's SIGNIFICANT OTHER?

V, better known by his stage name Kim Kim Tae-Hyung, is the only member of BTS about whom Big Hit Entertainment felt compelled to issue a statement. It was said that he was dating a fan by the name of Hi before the reports that he was dating Jennie from BLACKPINK gained traction. As a result of the singer's frequent usage of the words "Hi Nuna," everyone began to believe the claims.

Big Hit Entertainment said, however, that even though V and Hi have been in contact with one another, they are not dating and are instead simply friends, as things began to receive more and more attention as time went on.

WHO IS JUNGKOOK'S GIRLFRIEND?

According to many claims in the media, the member of BTS known as Jungkook is not currently in a relationship. In the past, rumors have circulated that he is romantically involved with K-pop artists Jeong Ye In of the band Lovelyz and Jung Chae Yeon from the group DIA.

In addition to that, it was rumored that he was dating CUBE trainee Ko So-Hyun, and fans still connect them using their nicknames. However, no information can be verified.

WHO IS JIN'S CURRENT SIGNIFICANT OTHER?

It was rumored that Jin was romantically involved with the comedienne Lee Gook Joo. After Jin complimented her in the liner notes for the first three BTS albums, speculation that the two were dating gained momentum. Fans have speculated that something is going on between the two of them even though they have not addressed the rumors publicly.

WHO IS THE WOMAN THAT RM IS DATING?

Fans erupted into a frenzy when they saw RM take a band off of his wedding finger. Although RM was able to avoid dating rumors for most of his career, fans were shocked when they saw him take the ring off. Before you jump to any assumptions, there is currently no information available about his upcoming wedding.

However, many different stories in the media assert that he was in a relationship in the year 2017. RM stated the following in an interview with Billboard regarding the album 'Love Yourself' by BTS: "I thought it was the right outro for this album because it is a range of emotions - I'm saying I met this person that I love, this person is the love of my life right now, and I'm saying that I was confused and I was looking for love and this world is complex."

WHO IS JIMIN DATING, IF ANYBODY KNOWS?

Multiple names have surfaced throughout these many years. Some time ago, it was reported that the Korean pop sensation was involved in a romantic relationship with another K-pop artist, Han Seung-Yeon from the group KARA. When they were advertising Mamma Mia, Han revealed to a portal that Jimin "caught her eye," although Jimin has not discussed the incident.

WHO IS THE LUCKY LADY IN SUGA'S LIFE?

We are all aware that Suga has achieved a level of celebrity that has never been seen before. He has always had a ton of work on his plate and only recently cooperated with PSY, who is also a famous Korean singer.

It would seem that he has not been on any dates due to his hectic schedule. At least, that is what he asserts. While Suga and the K-pop artist Suran were collaborating on the song "Wine," romantic rumors began to circulate about the two of them. Nevertheless, its impact was short-lived. Therefore, according to the book, Suga is not yet taken.

WHO IS J-SPECIAL HOPE'S LADY IN HIS LIFE?

It is reported that J-Hope, a member of BTS, discovered love before he became famous. But, alas, things didn't go as planned, and the two of them went their own ways. Aside from the speculations, this is the one story concerning J-dating Hope's life that has received the most attention.

Printed in Great Britain
by Amazon